YOUR KNOWLEDGE HAS VALUE

- We will publish your bachelor's and master's thesis, essays and papers

- Your own eBook and book - sold worldwide in all relevant shops

- Earn money with each sale

Upload your text at www.GRIN.com
and publish for free

Bibliographic information published by the German National Library:

The German National Library lists this publication in the National Bibliography; detailed bibliographic data are available on the Internet at http://dnb.dnb.de .

Imprint:

Copyright © 2018 GRIN Verlag
Print and binding: Books on Demand GmbH, Norderstedt Germany
ISBN: 9783668901421

This book at GRIN:

https://www.grin.com/document/458807

Stephen Grams

The Bullying Policy of Schools. An Analysis

GRIN Verlag

GRIN - Your knowledge has value

Since its foundation in 1998, GRIN has specialized in publishing academic texts by students, college teachers and other academics as e-book and printed book. The website www.grin.com is an ideal platform for presenting term papers, final papers, scientific essays, dissertations and specialist books.

Visit us on the internet:

http://www.grin.com/

http://www.facebook.com/grincom

http://www.twitter.com/grin_com

CONCORDIA UNIVERSITY CHICAGO
Doctoral Program in Health and Human Performance

Assignment Title: Bullying Policy Analysis
Date of Submission: 4/17/17
Assignment Due Date: 4/23/17

Course: Policy Analysis, EDL 7210

If 20.8% of school-age children were contracting a given disease, were suffering from any contagious ailment, doctors, parents, and the community would be frantic in their search for a cure. Every day that new children were victims would be one day too many. There is an epidemic that affects over 1 in 5 children, and that plague is bullying (PACER, 2016.) Analysis of 80 studies showed that 35% of 12 – 18-year-olds reported being part of traditional bullying and an additional 15% part of cyberbullying (PACER). With these children being the future of this nation, it is the responsibility of schools and other agencies that are designed to protect children to enact policies not only to stop bullying, but also to set forth guidelines both defining the problem and listing consequences.

Bullying is defined as "systematically and chronically inflicting physical hurt or psychological distress" (Walton, 2008) and "has the effect of doing any of the following: (1) substantial interference with a student's education, (2) creation of a threatening environment, (3) substantial disruption of the orderly operation of the school" (YYYY, 2008). This problem is not limited to the school day. Victims of bullying also suffer in after-school programs such as athletics. "[A] football player who is intimidating, dominating, and aggressive on the field earns respect from his teammates and coaches" (Steinfeldt, 2012). Granted, we coaches praise athletes who are fighters, who play hard, and who are not afraid to stand their ground in competition. But there is a place when a line must be drawn, where respect for and safety of both teammates and opponents takes precedence over hard-nosed competition. For that reason, the language of high school anti-bullying policies includes after-school activities and hold athletes to the same high standards to which they must adhere during academic classes.

The purpose of this essay is to compare and contrast two K – 12 school district bullying policies: Walton County School District in Florida and YYYY School District in Pennsylvania. Both of these are public school districts that officially enacted an anti-bullying policy in 2008 in response to the alarming number of bullying cases being reported across the United States. The comparison between the two policies will be made in terms of language, procedural steps and reporting, and the perceived effectiveness of the two policies in hopes to determine commonalities as well as differences that make each policy effective in its given district.

Policy Language

The first differences within the language of the two policies occurred immediately, in Section 1 or I of the policies (YYYY used Arabic numerals where Walton County used Roman); also immediately noted was the difference in length, with YYYY's at 3 pages and Walton County's at 12. Walton's (2008) policy, entitled "Bullying and Harassment" (only bullying is considered herein), stated that "the District upholds that bullying or harassment…is prohibted." YYYY's (2008) policy, entitled "Bullying/Cyberbullying," stated that "the Board prohibits bullying." While these concepts are functionally similar, the description of by whom bullying is banned may be based on the size and school composition of the district covered. YYYY is a rural Pennsylvania district comprised of three elementary schools, one middle school, and one high school, with a total enrollment of 2079 students (YYYYsd.net, 2017). Walton County spans a substantial portion of the Florida panhandle, and has multiple schools at each level: six elementary schools, three middle schools, and three high schools, plus three charter schools, two alternative education schools, and a career development school, with a total enrollment of 7200 students (walton.k12.fl.us, 2017). From a practical consideration based on size and district area, it is practical for the Board of YYYY School District to oversee 5 schools, where the District as a whole is required to monitor the 18 buildings that comprise Walton County School

District. Many of the differences in these policies can be traced back to the geographic and demographic differences between the districts themselves.

On the opening page, in fact, in the first section, each policy emphasized the role of a bullying policy in providing a safe place in which students can learn. YYYY desired to create a "safe, positive learning environment (YYYY, 2008) and Walton County to produce an "educational setting that is safe, secure, and free from harassment and bullying of any kind (Walton, 2008). Safety for students registered therein is a primary concern for every district; thus, the language of the policy in terms of safety concerns is similar regardless of the size of the district.

The description of acts classified by Walton County as bullying is provided in Section II. The list is very specific and included examples of occurrences such as social exclusion, threat, stalking, and physical violence, but also included the phrase "but is not limited to" before providing a list of these and other offenses. YYYY did not list acts, but instead described in Section 2 offenses categorized as "an intentional electronic, written, verbal, or physical act or series of acts directed at another student or students, which occurs in a school setting, that is severe, pervasive..." and has the effects described in the opening paragraph. (YYYY, 2008). The value of a specific description is arguable. A specific list allows an administrator to show a student his or her offense on paper and prove that it is indeed bullying. On the other hand, a vaguer, all-encompassing definition allows for case-by-case analysis and determination if an act is bullying or not in a given situation.

A notable difference in the language of the two policies comes from the inclusion of employees in the code for Walton County but not for YYYY. Walton County's policy reads; "The District upholds that bullying and harassment of any student or school employee is prohibited," (Walton, 2008) which recognizes not only that educators can bully but can be bullied by peers, superiors, and students as well. Bullying at the teacher/coach level at YYYY is covered in a separate document in the faculty handbook rather than in the same policy as the students; however, descriptions and consequences are similar.

Both districts provided a thorough description of the physical areas encompassed by the bullying policy. While both policies specified school grounds and any activities occurring there, as well as buses owned by the district regardless of location, the remainder of the descriptions differed somewhat. YYYY chose to describe cyberbullying in a separate section, grouping physical locations only here in Section 2, while Walton County included "use of data or computer software that is accessed through a computer, computer system, or computer network of a public K-12 education institution" in Section I, Part B (Walton, 2008). YYYY included district-issued bus stops as part of the included area; in the more rural areas of the district, many students spend an hour each morning traveling to a number of stops in their locale before finally arriving at the high school. A delay at any of those stops leaves the rest of the students on the route waiting for extended times, often in semi-secluded areas, hence, the rationale for including bus stops.

The language differed in to what the educational setting was referred. YYYY simply called all of its buildings collectively "the school," all locations "school grounds," and transportation including buses "school vehicles" (YYYY, 2008). Walton County described these areas as well, but referred to all of them in terms of "a public K-12 educational institution" (Walton, 2008). It seems as though this was written to include Walton County students who are at other districts for events such as athletic contests or as guests at dances or performances such as musical theater. Although the intentions behind this phrasing are good, it may in some cases be difficult to thoroughly investigate claims that have occurred within other districts. Likewise, YYYY made no mention of events occurring within other districts, unless those are accepted as covered under the term "school." Both parties may benefit from clarifying this section of the policy.

Expected behavior is described directly in the policy itself of the Walton County School District in Section III. "The Walton County School District expects students to conduct themselves as appropriate for their levels of development, maturity, and demonstrated capabilities with a proper regard for the rights and welfare of other students and school staff, the educational purpose underlying all school activities, and the care of school facilities and equipment" (Walton, 2008). YYYY provides its bullying policy to all students along with many others, including a description of expected behavior, in a Student Handbook on the first day of school; at the back of the handbook is a sign-off sheet with a place for the student's signature and a place for a parent's or guardian's signature which must be returned to the school promptly, signifying all students are then responsible for knowing and following the policies and expectations detailed within.

The reverse of what is described in the previous paragraph is true about descriptions of consequences listed within the policy. In Section IV, Walton County provided two ends of the spectrum and listed consequences as a range: "from positive behavior interventions up to and including suspension or expulsion, as outlined in the *Student Code of Conduct*" (Walton, 2008). YYYY (2008) listed specific consequences in Section 4, such as counseling, conference with parents, loss of school privileges, suspension, expulsion, and referral to a law enforcement agency. Positive behavior is described elsewhere for YYYY students (within the Handbook) and consequences are listed elsewhere for Walton County. As long as the entire picture is provided despite different locations, these portions of the policies appear fundamentally equivalent given that students are provided with all information. Both policies likewise described consequences for retaliation. Since bullies strive to strike fear in their victims, those who find out that they were reported by their victims to authorities may feel the need to strike back physically or mentally. Both YYYY and Walton County included prohibition of retaliation and descriptions of punishments that may arise, although the description provided by Walton County was much more thorough. Both also assured students who report bullying of confidentiality.

Finally, YYYY (2008) mentioned implementation of the policy (in Section 4) while Walton County did not: "The superintendent or designee shall develop administrative regulations to implement this policy." Meetings take place for the high school with students divided by grade level within the first two days of each school year. The meetings are run by the school principal, acting as the designee of the superintendent, in order to clarify expectations for the student body for the upcoming school year. In those meetings, a number of policies are discussed, and students are informed of their roles in these policies. Following the guidelines of the district superintendent, the high school principal is able to lay a framework for the bullying policy and appraise students of definitions, reporting, and consequences – in other words, of the implementation as it will occur in the building during that year. However, by requiring students to behave correctly and follow the policy, they are also aids in the implementation of the policy as well, and both districts specify good behavior and adherence within the policy. Although these policies both deal with bullying in public K – 12 school districts, many points of the language used differ greatly. In many cases, the regional, geographic, and demographic differences between the two locations necessitate variation in how policies are worded. What is practical when overseeing 5 schools is often not practical for overseeing 18, and vice versa. However, the policies do parallel each other in many ways, specifying stakeholder involvement, describing the role of students in implementation, and providing assurances of confidentiality. In general, both policies are written well to achieve the goal; however, small adjustments may be needed to make each of the policies more thorough.

Procedural Steps and Reporting

In terms of procedural steps and the reporting process for bullying offenses, the policies could not differ more. YYYY (2008) stated in Section 3, "The Board encourages students who have been bullied to promptly report such incidents to the building principal or designee." No description of reporting process, time frame, or even who qualifies as a designee is given. In most cases, students who are bullied end up in the guidance office, implying that the school's two guidance counselors would be designees, as well as the vice principal who is primarily in charge of day-to-day disciplinary actions. Students may also turn in anonymous bullying complaints in "Bully Boxes," which funnel to the guidance office as well. Procedure after that is not specified in the policy.

Walton County's policy was very specific in describing the steps by which bullying should be reported and what events occur following the report. Section V was devoted completely to the reporting process. This policy also mentioned a District designee to whom complaints are to be submitted whether in person or anonymously, and described a number of ways by which bullying may be reported (in person, in anonymous boxes, using a bullying hotline) and a myriad of people by whom reporting may occur (those involved, family members, observers, and school staff). This section also assured reporters of lack of retaliation by the school system: "Submission of a good faith complaint or report of bullying or harassment will not affect the complainant or reporter's future employment, grades, learning or working environment, or work assignments" (Walton, 2008).

Section VI continued to describe procedural concerns, detailing the investigation process used for each reported act of bullying or harassment, including steps of initiation, interview, evaluation of facts, and determination as to whether the act or acts qualify as bullying. Section VII examined whether or not the incident, once proven, was within the scope of the District; if not, the incident is referred to law enforcement agencies if necessary or reported to parents regardless. Despite lacking the procedural details present in the Walton County policy, the YYYY policy likewise described prosecution if necessary in section 5, with a possible consequence of bullying being "referral to law enforcement officials" (YYYY, 2008). Section VIII of the Walton County policy specifically described the process by which parents would be notified if their child was involved in a bullying incident, which also falls under the category of reporting and is also absent from the YYYY policy. The comparison between these two policies in terms of procedural details of reporting incidents is easy to make because all details are absent from YYYY's policy.

Components to Enhance YYYY's Policy

As compared to the 12-page policy adopted by Walton County School District, the 3page policy of the YYYY School District is obviously less complete and detailed based simply on length. At one-quarter of the length, there simply is no space for in-depth descriptions of any procedure within the YYYY policy. First and foremost, the most notable absence from YYYY's policy is a description of a detailed reporting process. No requirements for reporting nor steps for doing so are included whereas Walton County described the procedure from the initial report up to the point of a decision regarding punishment. Although the in-depth description provided by Walton County may not be necessary, a basic description of what is to occur if an incident is reported and subsequently proven would greatly enhance the policy. Walton County also provided a specific list of offenses that qualify as bullying but noted that offenses "may involve but is not limited to" those listed therein (Walton, 2008). Although the focus of this assignment is to compare bullying policies, the mention and description of harassment in the Walton County policy should be either included in this YYYY policy or in one of its own due to the relevance and interrelated nature of the two topics. All of these additional policy components would make the YYYY policy more complete.

What Would Not Be Effective for YYYY

While the majority of the components of this policy are effective for both schools, the language used in the policies differs. In many cases, the more specific policy presented by the Walton County School District speaks to the size of the district and the number of buildings that are overseen by a single governing school board. While a smaller district such as YYYY may be more able to deal with infractions on a case-by-case basis, larger districts require a very specific plan simply due to the number of disciplinary proceedings that may be occurring at a given time at any of several sites. Also, with a single high school of 690 students (adjacent to which the superintendent's office is located) and a single middle school, the majority of students are wellknown to the staff and administration, reducing the need for identification procedures within the reporting process. When most students know each other, many acts of bullying that occur are witnessed by individuals who know all parties involved. While this does not make the specificity of reporting ineffective per se, following each of Walton County's steps may delay the process when a condensed version of the same process would better serve the smaller district.

How the Policy is Communicated

As was mentioned previously, each student at the high school receives a Student Handbook at the beginning of the school year. Many policies for students, including attendance, dress code, and bullying are included therein. Students then attend grade level meetings within the first two days of school in order to discuss the information contained in the handbook as well as other disciplinary and practical concerns as well; some are grade level specific, such as graduation requirements for seniors and location of classrooms for freshmen, while some, like the bullying policy, apply across the board. Following that meeting, all social studies teachers review the handbook with their classes within the first week of school, going over the contents and specific details of the information contained within. At the back of the Handbook is a sign-off sheet, with one line for a student's signature and one for a parent's or guardians. At the high school level, the intent of this is for parents and students to go through the rules together, then the parent to provide a signature that both proves he or she reviewed the rules for the student to understand and that he or she has read the rules as well. This provides the district backing in case a parent claims he or she was unaware that what was done by a student was against the rules, or that the consequences of an action were unexpected. In addition to the copies provided to each student, each teacher is given a copy of the bullying policy and encouraged to hang it in his or her classroom so that students are reminded and aware of consequences and know about what steps can be taking if they are bullied or bullying. The school website likewise has an easily accessible link that provides many disciplinary or behavior poilicies; the bullying policy is available there as well. By offering so many opportunities to read, learn, and review this policy, the stakeholders to whom it matters have every reason to know it well and respect the positive atmosphere presented as ideal.

How Successful is the Policy?

While every school district has some incidents that occur year-to-year due to the number of students and developmental level present, the atmosphere at YYYY suggests that the bullying policy is predominantly successful. Within the past year, a few incidents have occurred. One involved a new student in the high school with Tourette's syndrome, but once all parties involved met with the high school principal to discuss what was occurring, both girls apologized, the bullier for what she had done and the bullied for the mean things she had said in retaliation. With stress management counseling, the young lady with Tourette's has greatly reduced symptoms and has made many friends at the high school. They are teammates on the track team now, with the young lady who was bullied far exceeding the bully in ability! Another young man was involved with a much more serious incident, and after the investigation was complete, the bully was suspended for half of the school year and it was debated as to whether he should be reported to law enforcement.

Although the policy stated that "the Superintendent or designee shall develop administrative regulations to implement this policy" and no specific steps were given, implementation has occurred and incidents are reported, processed, and mediated or punished as fits the individual circumstance, as is illustrated by the cases described above. Without having access to data regarding bullying reports and proven incidents both before and after the policy was enacted, it is not possible to state positively that the policy has or has not altered the frequency of occurrences. However, the manner in which bullying cases are handled is efficient and does strive to identify bullies and to protect victims. Evidence suggests that this policy, then, is effective.

How this Has Added to My Knowledge Base

Although I was familiar with our bullying policy before beginning this assignment, I had never considered how it compared in format and information to any other. During my undergraduate degree, when I was an education minor, we read many policies and learned much background information into major trends in education. Bullying was not a primary concern until many years later, and therefore I learned little regarding ideal formats and presentations of policies concerned with this topic. Similarly, I have little experience with policies of any sort that are issued by larger districts. Researching the demographics of Walton County School District and comparing its dynamics to that of the YYYY School District has been very informative in terms of the day-to-day differences that necessarily exist between a district with 18 schools and one with 5.

Despite the differences that exist between the policies, commonalities exist as well. Language that assures punishment, discourages false reports or repercussions, and encourages the creation of a safe and supportive school setting exists in both policies. This suggests that, in analyzing policies of any given sort, there will be a similar structure and organization on which the policy is based; analysis would then occur on the portions that differ. Before taking this course, I did not know that policies for such different demographic areas would be founded on the same base concepts. Comparing the sections of the two policies that dealt with similar topics illustrated this similarity in framework well.

Overall, this assignment and this course as a whole has taught me to consider not only policies, but the rationale behind each. The purpose of every policy stems from the demographics and motivation of the key stakeholders for whom it is written. By considering

not only the literal meaning of a policy but instead delving into the background information

behind it, a deeper appreciation for what it means to its key stakeholders and how it affects

them can be achieved. Although I have little previous experience in policy analysis, this

assignment and this course has well illustrated the procedure by which policies are analyzed as

well as the reasons for policies to be written in the manner in which they are.

References

PACER. 2016. PACER's national bullying prevention center. Retrieved from

http://www.pacer.org/bullying/resources/stats.asp

Steinfeldt, J. A., Vaughan, E. L., LaFollette, J. R., & Steinfeldt, M. C. (2012). Bullying among

adolescent football players: Role of masculinity and moral atmosphere. *Psychology of*

Men & Masculinity, 13(4), 340 – 353.

Walton County School District (2017). District info. Retrieved from

http://www.walton.k12.fl.us/district-info

Walton County School District (2008). Bullying and harassment. Retrieved from

https://blackboard.cuchicago.edu/bbcswebdav/pid-2579274-dt-content-rid-

8977161_2/courses/8286.201730/walton-policy-5-301.pdf

YYYY School District (2017). District statistics. Retrieved from

http://www.YYYYsd.net/district_statistics

YYYY School District (2008). Bullying/cyberbullying.